consumerfinance.gov

Doing business with the CFPB

A guide for small businesses

Consumer Financial
Protection Bureau

Table of contents

Message from Rich Cordray, Director of CFPB

Thank you for considering the Consumer Financial Protection Bureau (CFPB) for your future business opportunities. We are a new agency, created in 2011 as part of the Dodd-Frank Wall Street Reform Act, but we have a crucial mission: protecting the American consumer. We aim to be a model government agency that helps consumer finance markets work by making rules more effective, by consistently and fairly enforcing those rules, and by empowering consumers to take more control over their economic lives.

We value great people and excellent teamwork, and the Bureau is proud of the emphasis we place on partnering with small businesses in our contracting opportunities.

Our Office of Procurement and Office of Minority and Women Inclusion are fully committed to guiding small businesses through the procurement process to ensure utilization of small business services in support of protecting and serving the American consumer. It is our mission and responsibility to continue to develop and provide information and tools necessary to compete for business with the CFPB.

We look forward to working with your small business.

The Consumer Financial Protection Bureau (CFPB)

Who we are

- Founded as a result of the Dodd-Frank Wall Street Reform and Consumer Protection Act which was signed into law in July 2010
- Holds primary responsibility for regulating financial products and services aimed at the American consumer
- Has jurisdiction over banks, credit unions, securities firms, payday lenders, mortgage servicers, foreclosure relief services, debt collectors, and other financial services

What we do

- Write rules, supervise financial companies, and enforce federal consumer financial protection laws
- Restrict unfair, deceptive, or abusive acts or practices
- Take consumer complaints
- Promote financial education
- Research consumer behavior
- Monitor financial markets for new risks to consumers
- Enforce laws that outlaw discrimination and other unfair treatment in consumer finance

Message from the Office of Minority and Women Inclusion

Stuart Ishimaru, Director, Office of Minority and Women Inclusion

A primary mission of the Office of Minority and Women Inclusion (OMWI) at the CFPB is to increase the participation of minority- and women-owned businesses in the programs and procurements of the Bureau. OMWI partners with the Office of Procurement to provide guidance to small businesses on how to navigate the intricacies of federal contracting. We seek out diverse suppliers through active

involvement with small and minority-owned business trade organizations, community outreach efforts, and participation in trade organization events. We monitor and report our progress towards achieving our goals with an emphasis on continual improvement. We hope this guide will be a starting point to give you tools and support to do business with the CFPB. Visit www.consumerfinance.gov for the latest sourcing opportunities. We look forward to working with you and welcome your suggestions for improvements.

Message from the Office of Procurement

David Gragan,
Senior Procurement Executive

The Office of Procurement's mission is to serve as a steward of acquisition excellence among government agencies by reinventing processes to take full advantage of technology, transparency, open communications and best practices.

We are partnering with the Office of Minority and Women Inclusion to ensure that small businesses have the resources and opportunities to compete for work with the Bureau. As a proponent of partnering with small businesses, I look forward to working with your firm in the future.

Our commitment to small businesses

Our small business goals

As the main economic drivers and job creators in America, small businesses play a crucial role in the U.S. economy. The CFPB fully recognizes the importance of small businesses and is committed to partnering with them for contracting opportunities.

To ensure that small businesses receive a portion of federal procurements, Congress has established annual goals of 23% for the amount of contract dollars that should be directed towards different socioeconomic categories of small businesses. The CFPB, in its commitment to promoting small businesses, has individually set a higher goal of 28.5% and has significantly exceeded that goal in FY2011 and is on track to exceed that goal in FY2013.

CFPB vs. government small business dollars
(as a percentage of total eligible dollars FY11-FY13)

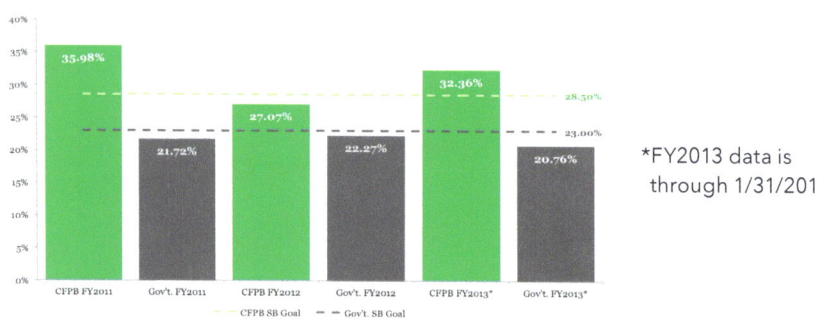

*FY2013 data is through 1/31/2013

Historical obligations by product/ service categories

In FY12, the CFPB used 78 different NAICS codes, but consulting services was the most common.

FY11 obligations by NAICS code

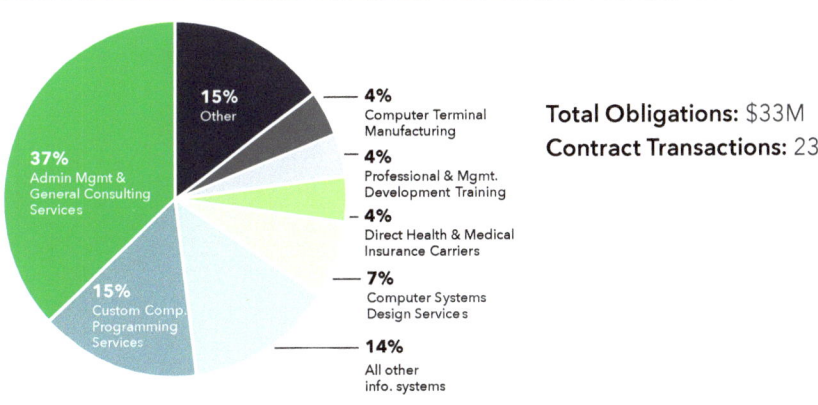

Total Obligations: $33M
Contract Transactions: 238

37% Admin Mgmt & General Consulting Services

15% Custom Comp. Programming Services

15% Other

4% Computer Terminal Manufacturing

4% Professional & Mgmt. Development Training

4% Direct Health & Medical Insurance Carriers

7% Computer Systems Design Services

14% All other info. systems

FY12 obligations by NAICS code

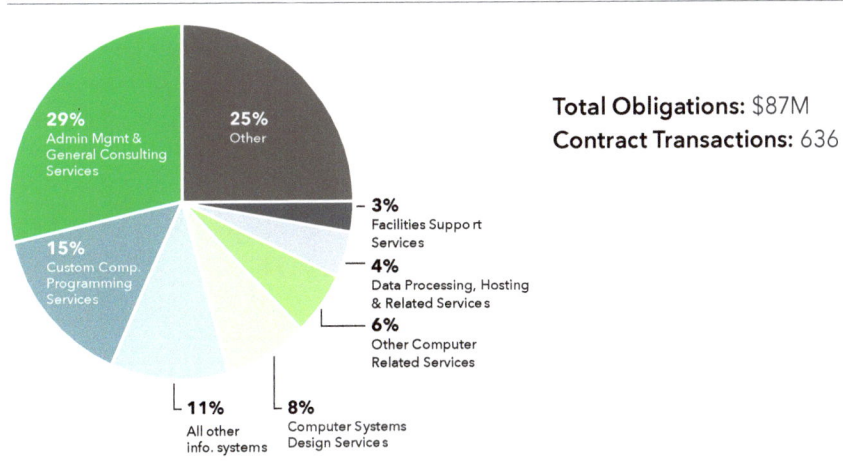

Total Obligations: $87M
Contract Transactions: 636

29% Admin Mgmt & General Consulting Services

25% Other

15% Custom Comp. Programming Services

3% Facilities Support Services

4% Data Processing, Hosting & Related Services

6% Other Computer Related Services

11% All other info. systems

8% Computer Systems Design Services

Where we are doing business

Each of 30 states acted as the principal place of performance, but DC, VA, and MD comprised over three-quarters of total action obligation dollars.

FY12 action obligations by principal place of performance

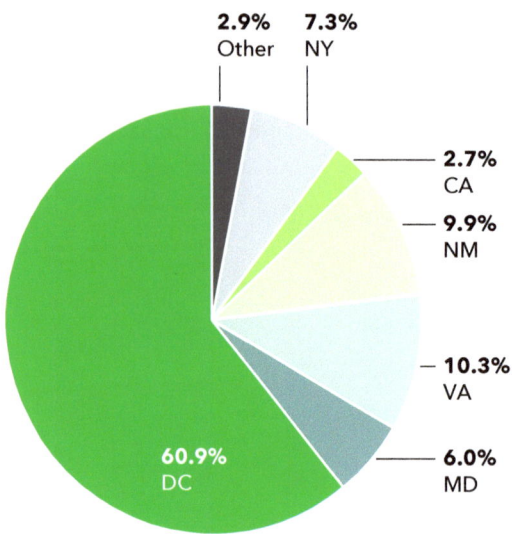

2.9% Other

7.3% NY

2.7% CA

9.9% NM

10.3% VA

6.0% MD

60.9% DC

NOTE: Data is pulled from FPDS and is meant to be a historical snapshot for informational purposes, not a predictor of future places of performance by the Bureau.

Total action obligations for FY2012 was $87.7M.

"Other" encompasses 24 other states including AL, AR, CO, CT, FL, GA, IL, IN, KY, LA, MA, MN, NC, NE, NH, NJ, OH, OK, OR, PA, SD, WI, TN and TX.

Opportunities

We openly communicate contract opportunities using a variety of government portals and websites.

1. Federal Business Opportunities (FedBizOpps)
2. General Services Administration (GSA) eBuy
3. Forecasted opportunities on www.consumerfinance.gov
4. SEWP (www.sewp.nasa.gov) for IT supplies

Finding opportunities and selling to the government

The acquisition process begins when an agency decides to seek goods or services from the private sector. The three most frequently used procurement methods utilized by the federal contracting community are:

- **Open Market Acquisitions** (unrestricted, and various **small business set-aside** competitions including 8(a) set-asides, are performed under this procurement method)
- **Purchase Card Programs**
- Orders from pre-existing contracting vehicles such as the **General Services Administration (GSA) Federal Supply Schedules**.

In addition, all small businesses should consider partnering with other firms to sell to the federal government; this is known as "subcontracting."

Open Market Acquisitions

Federal agencies can buy from outside vendors in a variety of ways. Competition among multiple companies for federal procurement opportunities helps ensure that the government will obtain the highest quality work at the best value.

Open market federal solicitations are published at www.FedBizOpps. gov, the federal government's procurement portal, which lists procurements valued over $25,000. Companies wishing to compete for an open market contract must submit a bid or proposal to do the work. The agency then selects the best offer and awards the contract to the winning firm.

Small Business Set-Asides

The Small Business Program helps assure that small businesses are awarded a fair proportion of government contracts by reserving certain government purchases exclusively for participation by small business concerns.

The determination to make a small business set-aside is usually made by the Contracting Officer (CO).

> ⚲ FedBizOpps is short for "Federal Business Opportunities." FedBizOpps can be accessed on the Internet at www.fbo.gov or www.FedBizOpps.gov. This site allows you to search for federal procurement opportunities valued over $25,000 and you can choose to receive automatic e-mails when procurements are announced.

Under the set-aside program, every acquisition of supplies or services that has an anticipated dollar value between $3,000 and $150,000 is automatically reserved for small businesses. Every set-aside requires that there be a reasonable expectation that offers will be obtained from two or more small business concerns that are competitive in terms of market prices, quality, and delivery. If one acceptable offer is received, the CO is required to make the award to that firm. If no acceptable offers are received, the set-side will be withdrawn, and goods or services will be solicited on an unrestricted basis.

For contracts over $150,000, the CO is required to set it aside if there is a reasonable expectation that offers will be obtained from at least two responsible small business concerns and that the award will be made at fair market prices. In some cases, the CO will first do market research by issuing a "Sources Sought" asking for small businesses to respond with a brief written statement of their qualifications to provide a particular good or service. If the CO determines that two competitive offers will be received, the procurement will be set aside. The agency can also set aside a procurement for a particular type of small business such as a HUBZone or SDVOSB.

Purchase Card

Federal government agencies began using the purchase card in the late 1980s as a way to acquire small-dollar items in a more efficient manner than open market acquisitions.

The Bureau does have a Purchase Card program where holders can go directly to the supplier or service provider for their micropurchase (i.e., under $3,000) needs.

GSA Schedules

Federal agencies often select potential vendors from the General Services Administration (GSA) Schedules, also referred to as Multiple Award Schedules or Federal Supply Schedules (FSS). Administered by the GSA, the schedules deliver millions of commercial supplies and services at volume discount pricing to government purchasers.

Whether your firm sells everyday items like cleaning supplies or provides specialized services like language translation or event planning, the schedules likely have a contract category that fits your business. To be listed on the GSA schedules, contractors must offer to sell their products or services to the government at what the GSA considers to be a fair and reasonable price. Federal agencies throughout the government may then buy from the vendor at the schedule-listed price or ask listed vendors to compete for specific procurements.

Becoming a schedule contractor is a multi-step process and can take several months to complete. More information: www.gsa.gov.

Sole Source Procurements

The government may also award a contract to a company without holding a competition. This kind of award is called a sole source and is available only under special circumstances (e.g., only one firm can perform the work, national security concerns) set out in federal law.

Subcontracting

Small firms can partner with other companies that have government contracts or are bidding as prime contractors. Smaller companies often fill niches that complement a prime contractor's services. Large firms bidding on contracts valued at $650,000 or more must submit an acceptable subcontracting plan that sets percentage (based on the contract's total value) and dollar goals for the award of subcontracts to small business, veteran-owned small business, service-disabled veteran-owned small business, HUBZone, small disadvantaged business and women-owned small business concerns.

Subcontracting can present small businesses with opportunities that might otherwise be unattainable because of limited resources, staffing, capital, or experience.

Working with the federal government

Definition of a small business

A small business is a sole proprietorship, partnership, corporation, or other legal entity that meets the following criteria:

- Is organized for profit

- Has a place of business in the United States

- Makes a significant contribution to the U.S. economy by paying taxes or using American products, materials or labor

- Does not exceed the numerical size standard* for its industry (see table below for commonly used services by the Bureau)

CFPB's commonly used services

Industry Group	Size Standard
Administrative management and management consulting services	$14.0M
Custom computer programming services / computer system design services	$25.5M
Facilities support services	$35.5M
Data processing, hosting, and related services	$30.0M

Source: Small Business Administration

*Size standards are based on revenues over a 3-year period or on number of employees.

A complete list of size standards can be found at http://www.sba.gov/sites/default/files/files/Size_Standards_Table(1).pdf.

Small business eligibility

Under the FAR, qualifying small businesses can receive preferences during the federal procurement process.

As mentioned previously, the CFPB and the other federal agencies establish annual goals for awarding contracts to small businesses. To help achieve these goals, the federal agencies use several preference programs authorized by the Federal Acquisition Regulation (FAR). However, to be eligible for these programs, a firm must first demonstrate that it is considered a "small business" according to the FAR.

⏺ What is the FAR?

Small businesses are highly encouraged to become familiar with the Federal Acquisition Regulation (FAR) before attempting to pursue federal contracts. The FAR is codified in Title 48 of the Code of Federal Regulations (CFR) and sets forth the requirements of contractors for selling to the government, as well as the rules for proposals and for the payment of invoices.

Part 19 of the FAR governs "Small Business Programs." This part describes programs giving preferences to small businesses to participate in federal procurements. You can read the FAR at www.acquisition.gov/FAR/.

Types of small businesses

Small businesses owned by socially and economically disadvantaged individuals can qualify for additional preferences in federal procurement.

Government agencies are required by law to award a percentage of contracts to small businesses. Agencies also set procurement goals for small, disadvantaged, HUBZone, woman-owned and service-disabled veteran-owned small businesses. To qualify as a small business under one of these socioeconomic categories, the company must fit the definitions set out by the Small Business Administration (SBA). These definitions are explained in the following pages.

Small Disadvantaged Businesses (SDB)

A small disadvantaged business is a small business that is owned and operated by one or more people that is considered socially and economically disadvantaged. An individual is considered "socially disadvantaged" if they have been subjected to prejudice or bias based on their racial or ethnic identity. Individuals are seen as "economically disadvantaged" if their ability to compete in the economy has been impaired due to diminished capital and access to credit.

Businesses self-certify that they are SDBs in order to make them eligible for benefits in federal procurement. There are three ways to become certified as an SDB:

- All firms that are current participants in the SBA's 8(a) Business Development Program are automatically deemed to be certified as SDBs

- Any firm may apply to the specific procuring agency stating they meet the eligibility standards of an SDB

- A procuring agency may accept a certification from another entity (e.g., a private certifying agency or a state or local government) that a firm qualifies as an SDB if the agency deems it appropriate.

African Americans, Native Americans, Hispanic Americans, Asian Pacific Americans and Subcontinent-Asian Americans are presumed to qualify. All individuals must have a net worth of less than $750,000 excluding the equity of the business and primary residence.

8(a) Businesses

Some certified SDBs may also qualify for participation in the SBA's 8(a) Business Development Program. This program helps SDBs compete in the federal and private sectors.

The focus of the program is to provide business development support such as mentoring, business counseling, training, financial assistance, surety bonding, and other management and technical assistance.

The major advantage of this program is that it allows the government to contract, on a noncompetitive basis, up to $4 million per contract ($6.5M for manufacturing) with 8(a) certified firms. Businesses must meet eligibility requirements established by the SBA each year.

Women-Owned Small Businesses (WOSB)

A women-owned small business is a small business that meets the following two conditions:

- At least 51 percent owned by one or more women, or, in the case of any publicly owned business, at least 51 percent of the stock is owned by one or more women
- Management and daily business operations are controlled by one or more women

Small businesses can self-certify with supporting documents or receive third-party certification with supporting documents.

Historically Underutilized Business Zone (HUBZone) Businesses

The HUBZone program stimulates economic development and creates jobs in urban and rural communities by providing federal contracting preferences to small businesses. These preferences go to small businesses that obtain HUBZone certification from the SBA.

To receive this certification, the firm must fill out an application that demonstrates that the firm meets the following criteria:

- It is a small business by SBA standards
- It is owned and controlled at least 51 percent by U.S. citizens, a Community Development Corporation, an agricultural cooperation, or an Indian tribe
- Its principal office is located within a HUBZone, which includes lands considered "Indian Country" and military facilities closed by the Base Realignment and Closure Act
- At least 35 percent of its employees reside in a HUBZone

In addition to determining which businesses are eligible to receive HUBZone contracts, the SBA maintains a listing of qualified HUBZone small businesses that federal agencies can use to locate vendors.

Service-Disabled Veteran-Owned Small Businesses (SDVOSB)

To qualify as a SDVOSB, a business must be at least 51 percent owned by one or more service-disabled veterans. If a veteran has a permanent service-connected disability and the firm is run by a spouse or permanent caregiver, the firm can still qualify for this status.

As with small businesses in general, the SBA places the responsibility for certifying whether a business is a SDVOSB on the firm itself. To qualify as a SDVOSB, the firm must self-certify that 1) at least 51 percent of the business is owned by one or more service-disabled veterans and 2) management and daily business operations are controlled by one or more service-disabled veterans.

Self-certification for SDVOSBs can be supported by the presentation of a Defense Department Form 214 which states the owner has a service-connected disability and a letter from the U.S. Department of Veteran Affairs (VA).

Contracts are awarded through a sole-source or set-aside based on competition restricted to SDVOSBs (outlined in FAR 19.1405 and 19.1406).

Veteran-Owned Small Businesses (VOSB)

To qualify as a Veteran-Owned Small Business, a business concern must be at least 51 percent owned by one or more eligible veterans, or, in the case of any publicly owned business, at least 51 percent of the stock is owned by one or more veterans and whose management and daily business operations are controlled by such veterans.

Certification requirements for different types of small businesses

Type of Small Business	Entity responsible for certification	Certification procedure
General small business	Self-certification	Register on SAM Register on SBA
SDB, 8(a), HUBZone	SBA	Complete application form on SBA
WOSB	Self-certification*	Register on SAM Register on SBA
SDVOSB	Self-certification	Be able to produce DD-214 if contested, as well as receive disability rating from VA

*WOSBs may self-certify or elect to use the services of these SBA-approved Third Party Certifiers to demonstrate eligibility.

El Paso Hispanic Chamber of Commerce (http://www.elpaso.org/)†
National Women Business Owners Corporation (http://www.nwboc.org/)†
US Women's Chamber of Commerce (http://www.uswcc.org/)†
Women's Business Enterprise National Council (WBENC) (http://wbenc.org/)†

† The nongovernmental websites in this document are provided for informational purposes only and do not represent the official views of the CFPB or other Federal government agencies.

Steps required of small businesses to do work with the federal government

To become eligible for a small business preference, a firm must:

❶ Get a DUNS identification number

DUNS stands for Data Universal Numbering System. It is a system developed and regulated by Dun & Bradstreet (D&B) and is recognized as a universal standard for identifying and tracking over 100 million businesses worldwide. To get a DUNS number, contact D&B at (888) 814-1435 or visit www.dnb.com/us.

❷ Register on the System for Award Management (SAM)

SAM combines federal procurement systems and the Catalog of Federal Domestic Assistance into one new system. This consolidation is being done in phases. The first phase of SAM includes the functionality from the following systems:

- Central Contractor Registry (CCR)
- Federal Agency Registration (Fedreg) Online Representations and Certifications Application
- Excluded Parties List System (EPLS)

3 Register with the Small Business Administration (SBA)

The SBA is a United States government agency that provides support to entrepreneurs and small businesses. More details about these steps can be found in the following pages.

The proposal process for contracting opportunities

Follow the four high-level steps below to start the proposal process for open contracting opportunities:

1 **Register**	Register with the System for Award Management (SAM) and Small Business Administration
2 **Identify**	Identify your company based on any applicable small business categories including small disadvantaged, women-owned, service-disabled veteran-owned, and/or historically underutilized business zones
3 **Contact**	Contact the Office of Procurement to introduce your company and its business capabilities
4 **Respond**	Respond to a CFPB request for information, proposal, quotation, or response

> 💬 Register with SBA and SAM to gain eligibility on contract vehicles through the General Services Administration (GSA) Federal Supply Schedule (FSS) and National Aeronautics and Space Administration (NASA) Solutions for Enterprise-Wide Procurement (SEWP).

Registering with SAM

All government contractors must be registered on the System for Award Management (SAM).

How to Register

To register at http://www.sam.gov/portal/public/sam you will need the following information:

- Obtain a Data Universal Number System (DUNS) Number from http://fedgov.dnb.com/webform

- Obtain a Federal Tax ID Number, Employer ID Number (EIN), and Taxpayer ID Number (TIN) from http://www.irs.gov

- Identify NAICS code(s) based on business capabilities at http://www.census.gov/eos/www/naics

- Identify Standard Industrial Classification (SIC) code(s) based on business capabilities at http://osha.gov/pls/imis/sicsearch.html

- Provide a bank account number and routing number for electronic payments

Registering with the SBA

If you own a small business, you should register with Small Business Administration (SBA) for all possible NAICS codes.

How to Register

To register at http://www.sba.gov you will need the following information:

- Select a legal business structure
- Register your business name at http://www.sba.gov/content/register-your-fictitious-or-doing-business-dba-name
- Obtain a Federal Tax ID Number and EIN from http://www.irs.gov
- Register with your state revenue office
- Register for business licenses and permits

⊙ The SBA provides some very helpful online resources for small firms that can be accessed anytime:

- Government Contracting Classroom at http://www.sba.gov/gcclassroom
- Contract Responsibilities at http://www.sba.gov/content/contract-responsibilities

Getting a GSA FSS contract

Your business is eligible to obtain a GSA Federal Supply Schedule (FSS) contract once you have registered with SAM and SBA.

How to Register

To register at http://www.gsa.gov/gettingonschedule you will need the following information:

- Get a DUNS Number from http://fedgov.dnb.com/webform
- Complete the Readiness Assessment for Prospective Offerors at www.vsc.gsa.gov/RA/ReadinessAssessment.pdf
- Past Performance Evaluation – Register with Open Ratings and provide contact information for 6 to 20 of your customers www.ppereports.com
- Obtain a GSA FSS contract and then respond to a solicitation

> ○ NAICS stands for North American Industry Classification System. It is the standard numbering system used by North American businesses and government to classify business establishments by their economic activity or process of production.

Becoming a SEWP prime contract holder

If you offer information technology supplies, becoming a SEWP prime contract holder is highly encouraged.

About SEWP

Solutions for Enterprise-Wide Procurement (SEWP) is a Government-Wide Acquisition Contract (GWAC) comprised of a set of pre-competed contracts.

It is managed by the National Aeronautics and Space Administration (NASA) and authorized by the U.S. Office of Management and Budget (OMB).

Prime contract holders are not added after the initial competition and award. Register at http://www.sewp.nasa.gov.

Additional resources

Organization	Website
U.S. Department of Commerce: BusinessUSA	www.business.usa.gov
U.S. General Services Administration	www.gsa.gov
U.S. Department of Treasury: Small Business Lending	www.treasury.gov/osdbu
U.S. Department of Veteran's Affairs	www.va.gov
Small Business Administration	www.sba.gov
Small Business Counseling	www.score.org†
Small Business Innovation Research	www.sbir.gov
Minority Business Development Agency	www.mbda.gov
Regional Small Business Development	www.knowyourregion.org†
Startup America	www.startupamerica partnership.org†

💬 Get training from Procurement Technical Assistance Centers (PTACs). They provide local, in-person counseling and training services for small business owners and are designed to provide technical assistance to businesses that want to sell products and services to the government. PTAC services are available either free of charge, or at a nominal cost. Find out more at http://www.sba.gov/content/procurement-technical-assistance-centers-ptacs.

Top ten tips for doing business with the CFPB

Here are some helpful tips, gathered from this guide, to help you successfully do business with the Bureau.

1. Familiarize yourself with the Bureau, its objectives and goals, and its business needs.

2. Know which small business concerns (e.g., SDB, WOSB, etc.) your firm can qualify for.

3. Get a DUNS number.

4. Register on SAM and SBA.

5. Learn about NAICS codes and figure out which ones may apply to your business.

6. Become a schedule contractor on GSA FSS.

7. Check FedBizOpps for opportunities and look for forecasted opportunities on our website.

8. Market your company's goods and services towards federal socio-economic goals and initiatives.

9. Do not hesitate to contact the CFPB's Office of Procurement at CFPB_Procurement@cfpb.gov with questions and concerns.

10. Be responsive to requests for additional information.

For more information, email:

cfpb_procurement@cfpb.gov
cfpb_omwi@cfpb.gov